BUG LIFE CYCLES

By Rod Barkman

BUTTERFLY

KidHaven PUBLISHING

Published in 2027 by
KidHaven Publishing, an Imprint of Greenhaven Publishing, LLC
2544 Clinton St., Buffalo, NY 14224

Written by: Rod Barkman
Edited by: Noah Leatherland
Designed by: Dan Scase

All facts, statistics, web addresses, and URLs in this book were verified as valid and accurate at time of writing. No responsibility for any changes to external websites or references can be accepted by either the author or publisher.

Cataloging-in-Publication Data

Names: Barkman, Rod.
Title: Butterfly / Rod Barkman.
Description: Buffalo, NY : KidHaven Publishing, 2027. | Series: Bug life cycles | Includes glossary and index.
Identifiers: ISBN 9781534571006 (pbk.) | ISBN 9781534571013 (library bound) | ISBN 9781534571020 (ebook)
Subjects: LCSH: Butterflies--Juvenile literature. | Butterflies--Life cycles--Juvenile literature.
Classification: LCC QL544.2 B37 2027 | DDC 595.789156--dc23

Printed in China

CPSIA compliance information: Batch #QS27KH: For further information contact Greenhaven Publishing LLC at 1-844-317-7404.

Please visit our website, www.greenhavenpublishing.com. For a free color catalog of all our high-quality books, call toll free 1-844-317-7404 or fax 1-844-317-7405.

Find us on

PHOTO CREDITS

All images are courtesy of Shutterstock.com, unless otherwise stated.

Recurring – rachel epley design, Anastasiia Hevko. Cover – Duncan Andison, Butterfly Hunter. 4–5 – Charlotte Ulrich, Krakenimages.com, Volodymyr TVERDOKHLIB, VH-studio, Andrii Iemelianenko, Prostock-studio. 6–7 – Yans Project, TZIDO SUN. 8–9 – jakrit yuenprakhon, Lapis2380, Sendo Serra. 10–11 – Tommy Daynjer, Guillermo Guerao Serra, Johan Larson. 12–13 – Mrs. Minard, Nilanka Sampath, Indokelana. 14–15 – Mike Redmer, 24Novembers. 16–17 – Nancy Ann Bowe, mountainpix. 18–19 – Russell Marshall, Leo Rosedahl, ANTHONY PAZ, Burdos. 20–21 – Rudmer Zwerver, Sukamoto. 22–23 – Jay Ondreicka, Leena Robinson, Manuel Balesteri, I Wayan Sumatika.

CONTENTS

Words that look like <u>this</u> can be found in the glossary on page 24.

LEARNING LIFE CYCLES

All living things have a life cycle. This is the changes they go through during their lives. A life cycle includes the start of life, growth, reproduction, and death.

Humans begin their lives as babies and grow into toddlers, children, and then teenagers. When humans become adults, they may have babies of their own before becoming elderly. This continues the human life cycle.

TEENAGER

ADULT

ELDERLY

MEET THE BUTTERFLY

Butterflies are flying insects. They have three main body parts—the thorax, the abdomen, and the head. Butterflies also have six legs and four wings. Butterfly wings are often very colorful.

It is believed that there are more than 19,000 types of butterflies in the world. Each of these butterflies is different. However, they all share a similar life cycle.

EGG

The life cycle of a butterfly starts with an egg. Inside each egg, a caterpillar starts to grow. Butterflies usually lay their eggs on plants that the caterpillars can eat after they hatch.

Some butterflies lay clusters of eggs. Some only lay one egg at a time.

Butterfly eggs can be round or oval-shaped. The type of butterfly that the eggs come from affects the color and texture of the eggs.

CATERPILLAR

The caterpillar eats its way out of the egg. It usually eats the rest of the egg before it begins eating the plant it hatched on. This plant is known as the host plant.

The caterpillar needs to eat to get ready for the next stage of its life cycle.

Caterpillars are the larval stage of the butterfly's life cycle. They have a hard exoskeleton outside their bodies to protect them. Exoskeletons do not grow, so the caterpillar must shed its exoskeleton as it gets bigger.

Caterpillars usually shed their exoskeletons around five times as they grow.

CHRYSALIS

The caterpillar stops eating when it has grown enough. It then attaches itself to a twig, leaf, or other object with silk. Then the caterpillar sheds its exoskeleton one more time to reveal the chrysalis.

a caterpillar preparing a chrysalis

Inside the chrysalis, a caterpillar changes into a butterfly. Most of its <u>organs</u> and other body parts become like liquid and turn into the body parts of a butterfly.

BREAKING OUT OF THE CHRYSALIS

When the butterfly has fully formed, the chrysalis splits open. The butterfly's wings are soft, wrinkly, and wet when it first breaks out of the chrysalis.

The butterfly pushes a special liquid from its body into its wings. This straightens out the wings and strengthens them. Once the butterfly's wings are dry, it is ready to fly.

HOW BUTTERFLIES LIVE

Once the butterfly's wings are strong enough, it flies away to look for a mate. Butterflies get food from flowers. Some butterflies feed on a sweet liquid made by plants, called nectar.

Butterflies are known for their colorful markings. These markings help butterflies find mates and protect themselves from predators. The colors and patterns on their wings can camouflage them or even scare predators away.

TYPES OF BUTTERFLIES

Butterflies can be found on every continent, except for Antarctica. These are just a few butterflies found around the world.

BRIMSTONE BUTTERFLY

can live for up to a year as an adult

QUEEN ALEXANDRA'S BIRDWING

the largest butterfly in the world

88 BUTTERFLY

has unique markings that look like two figure eights

the smallest known butterfly in the world

WESTERN PYGMY BLUE

END OF LIFE

Like all living things, a butterfly's life will come to an end. Butterflies have short lifespans. Most butterflies live for only two to four weeks. However, some kinds can live longer.

A butterfly's life may end because of old age or because of predators. But if the butterfly has mated before its death, the female will lay new eggs. This continues the life cycle.

LIFE CYCLE OF A BUTTERFLY

A butterfly changes a lot over the different stages of its life cycle.

A butterfly egg hatches into a caterpillar. The caterpillar eats until it is big enough and makes a chrysalis. Inside the chrysalis, the caterpillar changes into a butterfly. The butterfly then finds a mate.

GLOSSARY

camouflage the ability to blend in with the surroundings

hatch to break out of an egg

host an animal or plant that another creature lives on or in

larval relating to the young form of an insect

mate a partner (of the same species) that an animal chooses to produce young with

organs parts of the body that usually have a specific task

predators animals that hunt other animals for food

reproduction making more of the same type of thing

texture the feel and appearance of a surface

INDEX